Elegant Sister, What Happened?

There is Hope — A Guide For Healing Broken Women Behind Bars And In The Free World

A STEP-BY-STEP GUIDE TO EMPOWERMENT

GEORGIA HORTON

Professional Publishing House
1425 W. Manchester Ave. Ste B
Los Angeles, California 90047
323-750-3592
Email: professionalpublishinghouse@yahoo.com
www.Professionalpublishinghouse.com

Cover design: TWA Solutions
First Printing: January 2016
978-0-9861557-7-2
Library of Congress Control Number: 2015959864
10987654321

For inquiries contact the publisher: professionalpublishinghouse@yahoo.com

www.ingramcontent.com/pod-product-compliance
Lightning Source LLC
Chambersburg PA
CBHW080518110426
42742CB00017B/3161

About the Author

Georgia Horton, a woman who has suffered many traumatic experiences since the age of seven, has been bent but not broken. While drowning in the sea of despair and hopelessness, Georgia's faith in God became her life jacket.

Georgia was a lifer; she spent twenty-five years in prison. While incarcerated and since being in the free world, Georgia has been sharing her history and a reflection of the bad choices she made that led to her incarceration, with hopes of deterring youth from making the same or similar mistakes. She is a Youth Diversion Specialist in domestic violence and sexual assault. Georgia has participated in speaking to approximately 7,500 students (up to eighteen conferences with youth ranging in ages 12-18) in the Youth Diversion Program.

Ms. Horton has a heart for the wounded and her empathetic passion for women and men who are hurting causes her to make a profound impact on the lives of those who hear her speak — they always want more of her wisdom. She developed a curriculum manual while in prison, *Sister What Happened?* This manual centers on trauma-induced circumstances and criminality. The program focuses on helping those seeking insight through self-awareness. The program was so successful that one month after her release, she was allowed to return to share with those she left behind the prison walls — this was unprecedented and a miracle.

Georgia's new book, ELEGANT SISTER, WHAT HAPPENED? *There Is Hope – A Guide For Healing Broken Woman Behind Bars And In The Free World* is a must-read for all who seek to look inside themselves and who are honestly ready to change their life. This book is a mirror of reflections and a catalyst for change.

Georgia is available for speaking engagements, radio and television interviews.

CONTENTS

Foreword

By Dr. Rosie Milligan

This book is derived from a curriculum developed by the author, Georgia Horton. It was written while she was doing a life sentence; whereas she did twenty-five years at a women's prison in Chowchilla, California.

This curriculum was taught to and has helped many women behind bars to face and erase the negative thoughts and feelings about themselves and enabled them to move from beneath the shadow of disconnect from reality into a journey of true reflections. These women started seeing themselves and defining themselves apart from their circumstances that landed them behind bars.

Unprecedented, Georgia was allowed to return to the prison she was released from a few months after her release to, again, motivate and encourage those women she left behind. Upon Georgia's release, she hit the pavement running…looking for broken women and men in the *"free world"* that she could inspire via sharing her experience of rising from the ashes like a phoenix.

This is a self-help, self-evaluation tool, and a blueprint for guiding broken, beat down, cast down, locked down, and hurting women due to whatever nature or cause to overcome adversities and rise above their circumstances.

I asked Georgia, *"How does it feel to be free?"* She replied, *"Freedom does not come from being released from behind bars; rather, from your spirit. It was the discovery of WHO I AM apart from what I had come to be and after I had forgiven "all" those who participated in bringing trauma into my life."*

After reading this manual and having lengthy conversations with Georgia, listening to her speak at various events, it became crystal clear to me that the information in this book is needed and is necessary for helping to mend women behind bars and those in the free world whose lives have been shattered. Thus I present to you….
Elegant Sister, What Happened?

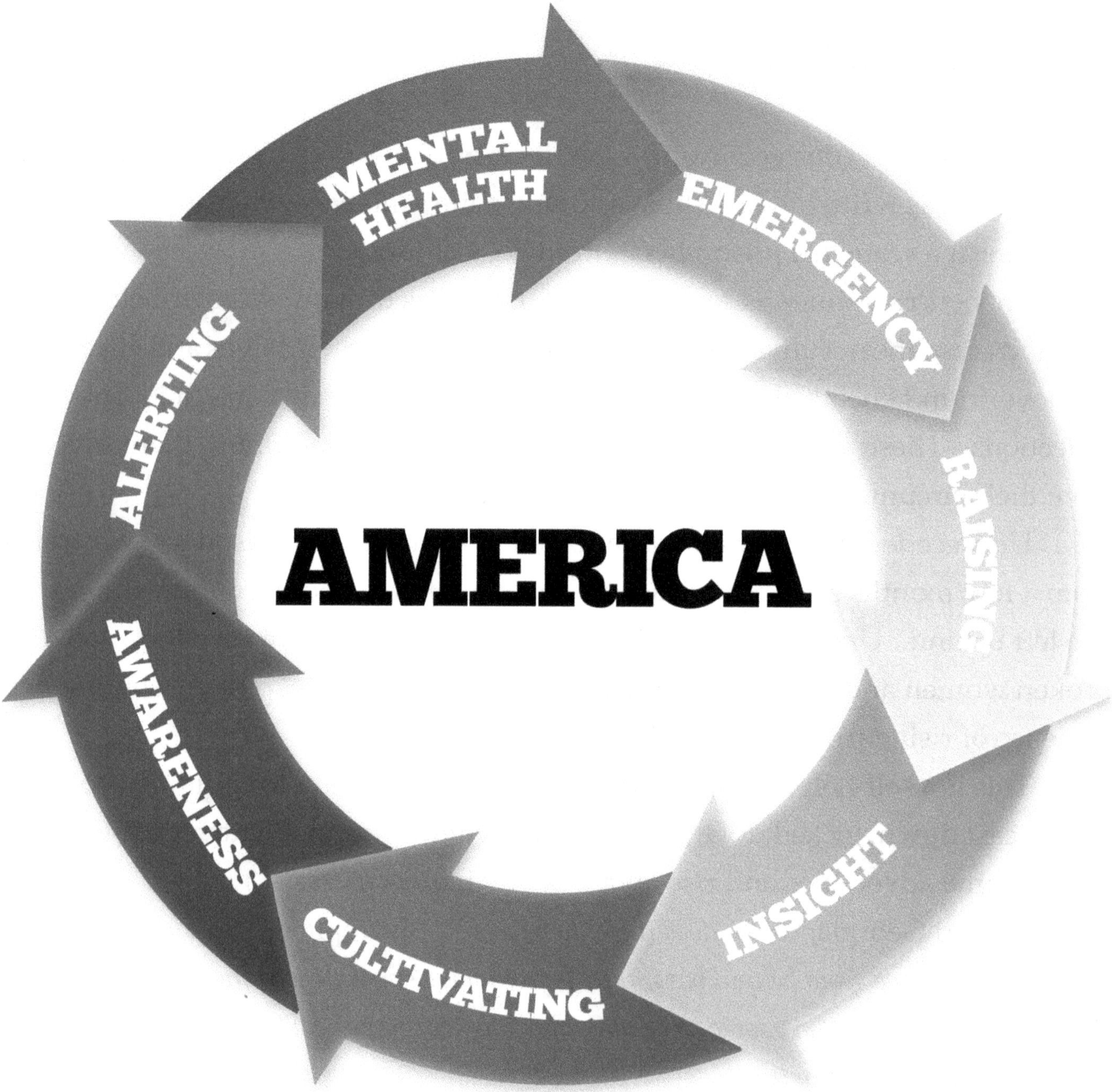
MENTAL HEALTH
EMERGENCY
RAISING
INSIGHT
CULTIVATING
AWARENESS
ALERTING
AMERICA

WHAT HAPPENED?

Mental Health and Mental Health Illness

There is a Difference

U nderstanding the difference between mental health issues and mental illness is one of the biggest breakthroughs in raising awareness that society, as a whole, can receive. Mental health is an issue that can happen in many people's lives for different reasons—a child that witnessed the death of a parent; someone who was in a serious, life-threatening car accident; or a person who returned home to an intruder. Trauma can enter our lives in many different ways. In fact, mental illness is a common diagnosis in women who were mentally, physical, and emotionally battered as a child or adult. Someone going through such issues can develop mental health issues unknowingly.

Because of this, people could go years without detecting mental illness. Let's face it, we tend to deal with these issues very lightly and address it, or refer to it, as it being "just life." We don't take the time to process it. We casually suppress it, not realizing everything that happens to us affects us — good or bad. By bringing awareness of the effects and symptoms of these issues, it is my hope that you will see the necessity of raising awareness, and bring this program into your churches, schools, drug programs, halfway houses, youth programs, foster homes, and correctional institutions. In the next few pages, I want to spend time identifying mental health issues in your environment.

Identifying Mental Health in Your Environment

20,000 Total

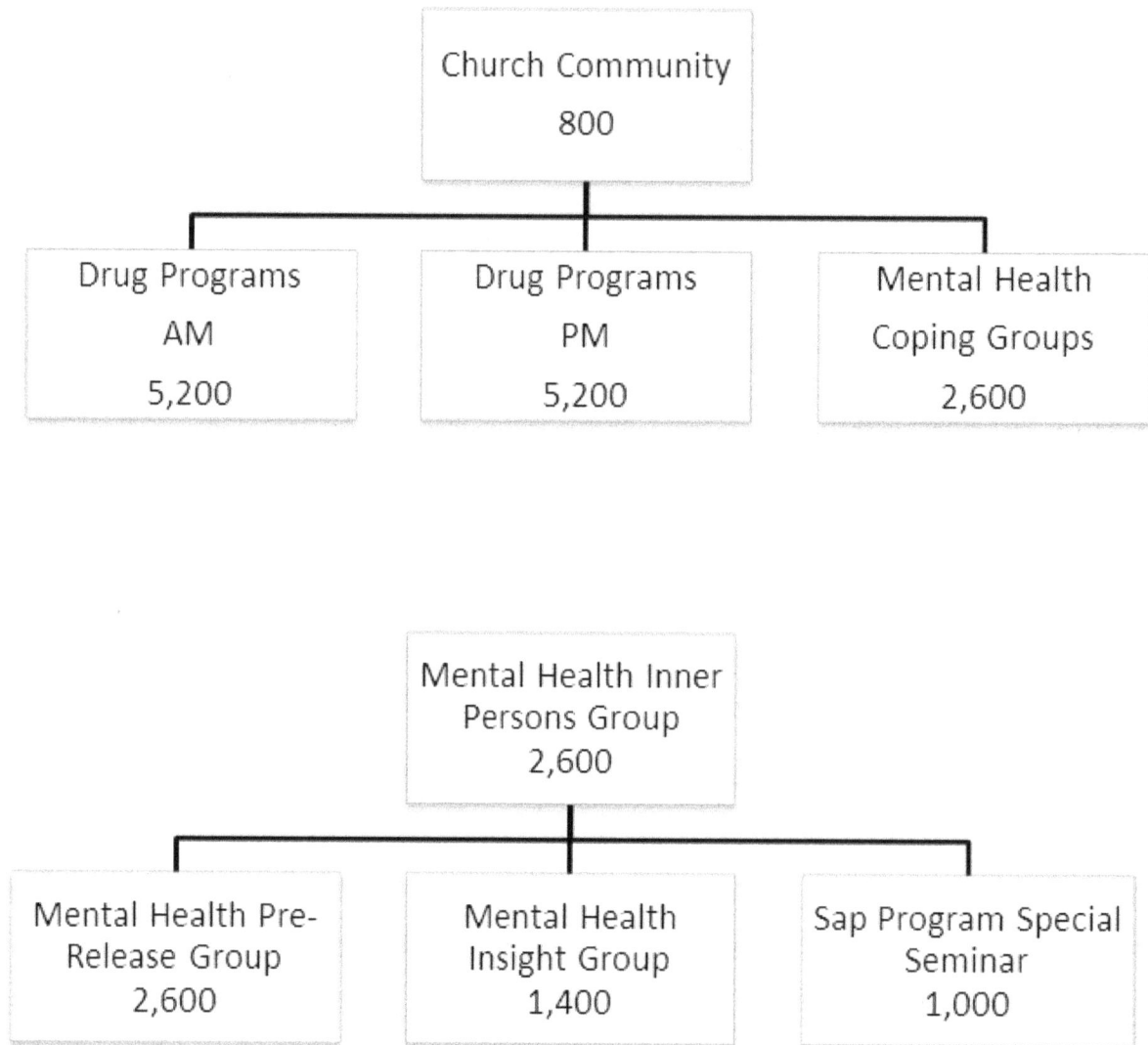

New System Igniting Generational Hope Together

Demographics show an alarming crisis in America today. Society sweeps mental health issues under the carpet because of the stigma produced by shame, helplessness, and the likes of awareness, but most of all fear. Fear has gripped the hearts of millions of families around the world. I understand that this emotion can take over one's thought pattern, because fear gripped me when fear entered my household and touched two members of my family, without permission. It came without warning, sound, indication, alarm, or a hint of its entry. Still, it came and took my loved ones without permission, and without my saying good-bye. Without closure or understanding, it left me with a loved one whose mental environment was unfamiliar.

Therefore, I understand that fear and helplessness, coupled with emotions of frustration, can cause anger at some point. But, even though mental illness affects the mind, body, and soul, it cannot transcend the spirit. The spirit is the courage, character, fortitude, and strength of mind. It is on this level of insight and revelation that we will embrace on this journey.

There are many different levels, but our goal and purpose is to meet and assist you on all levels, whether mental health or mental illness. We will tackle the hard, unspoken issue that is being hidden in our communities today. You are not alone in this anymore. As we go through this curriculum together, we will discover many different layers of trauma and pains and where disconnection is very present.

This level of disconnection is very dangerous. However, when you recognize the disconnect and embrace it, the more you start to feel better internally. The misdiagnosis of this feeling to be something that is good comes with the relief of pain and is not associated with any other identification. This new emotion called "disconnection" starts seeping into other areas of your life.

Disconnection makes it hard to address this issue on an emotional level at the beginning of treatment. First, you must address it on an intellectual level, dealing with it by looking or addressing it as another person. The damaged person has disconnected in order to survive. This person in you will not reconnect until she feels safe again. That is why, at the beginning of this journey, I asked, "How did you get here?" I was not referring to your location, but the place in your thought patterns.

Mirrors of Reflection

Exercise One

Dimension of Reflection

In this first step of embracing the mirror of reflection exercise, it's vital that you grasp this concept, knowing how to analyze, identify, and separate the perception of your reflections. This part gets complex — looking in the mirror and separating the dimensional views that are being revealed. You must embark upon them separately. Take your time to self-evaluate each dimension of your life.

Initial Viewpoint!

At first glance, while looking into the mirror of reflection, we perceive our physical appearance. The part we focus on mostly is how we identify ourselves. For example, a woman could find herself-worthy in the beauty of her hair, eye color, or frame. For a man, his muscles, biceps and triceps, or the way he grooms himself. Even though I address these positive aspects of the physical appearance, which can produce a good feeling if we allow these perceptions of one to speak to our very existence, it can be tragic because they are subject to change. Therefore, keep in mind, it can also produce a negative viewpoint of self, altering one's thought pattern of identification.

Examples may include thinking you're not pretty enough, too fat or skinny, short or tall, or not handsome enough. By allowing this aspect of reflection to speak to the core of your existence is a false imitation of one self. Before going on to your next level of reflection, let me make it clear that there is nothing wrong with being healthy and well groomed. We are speaking on a deeper level of identifying one's self with these aspects of life. These are where one's belief systems produce thought patterns of who we are, based on our outer man.

We must get past this surface in order to deal with the emotional part of us that has allowed us to make unhealthy decisions.

First Dimension of Reflection

What do you see?

Now we address the first dimension of the mirror of refection, the emotional part of us. For some, because the trauma that has been introduced in our lives, it's the only part of ourselves with which we can identify. Depression, anxiety, rejection, among other trauma-induced emotions, can take such a position in our soul that we are living life based on decisions from our emotional viewpoint. We place these emotions on a level of identifying ourselves by making the following statements:" I am depressed" and "I am insufficient" The list of negative, self-defeating talk could go on.

Instead of saying, "I feel depressed," or "I feel insufficient," we have to condition ourselves to give these affirmations and our emotions power over our lives by placing them in an identification viewpoint. You are not what you feel. Don't be discouraged or get overwhelmed, these are common occurrences in our thought pattern. As we gain insight and process these thought patterns, they will be replaced.

Remember that it took time for us to grasp the complexities of the brain and the function of mankind's thought patterns. They can be tricky. Why? Because the brain is a powerful instrument designed to pick up and store data. So be long-suffering with yourself, you deserve it.

Exercise One

We must separate and identify our emotional condition. What do you see when you look inside the mirror? We must take an honest look into our inner self and in doing this, we are able to separate our emotions from the real self. The real self that has been hurt and damaged by the trauma that comes into our lives through our circumstances.

Don't be afraid to look at that person. Don't allow the voice of your emotions to deceive you and tell you what you are feeling is who you are. Remember, you are not what you feel. In this exercise, I will be sharing the trauma of my past which resulted in the circumstances in my personal life.

Before we begin, I want you to know that the mirror you're looking into is mine. Yes, these are all the emotions I had to face in my mirror of reflection. Welcome to the first exercise.

Author's Testimony

Raised in a very dark place, where the atmosphere produced fear, disillusion, rejection, loneliness, neglect, and abuse, by age six, my innocence had already been robbed and violated by the very people whom, I believed, were closest to me. Today, I identify them as shadows. At thirteen, seven male shadows and one female shadow touched me. Those shadows violated me frequently, and because of who they were in my life, they got away with it being undetected.

So, in order for me to exist in this environment, I had to disconnect from myself—survival mode. Finally being tired of everyone else using my body for their own personal relief, I felt it was time for me to get something out of the deal. I started using my body to obtain favors. During that time, I met my first boyfriend and became pregnant. When he found out, he left and I have never seen him again. That left me feeling deserted, abandoned, disappointed, and insecure.

When my mother found out, she, fearing the wrath of my father, forced me to hide my pregnancy. When I was seven months pregnant, and it was clearly evident I was pregnant, my mother wrapped my stomach in the morning to hide it from the public's eye. The only contact my mother and me had during that time was her rapping me in the morning and her unwrapping me at night. I became very depressed and timid, believing I had no self-worth or value.

The day I went into labor, I was in a dark room with my sister. She put a pillow on my face to muzzle my screams so my father could not hear my cries. I had to wait until he left the house before I was taken to the hospital to have my baby. After all that, my child couldn't even come home with me. My mother forced me to give my son away. I slipped into a deep, delusional state in order to deal with my world. I became more and more disconnected, eventually running away from home and hitting the streets. I lost myself in prostitution.

Instructions

Take fifteen minutes to meditate on the message in the mirror. Then, on a separate sheet of paper, write down the words that apply to you. Please don't worry; no one is going to look at your paper unless you want them to see it. This is strictly about you and your journey. Also remember, this is my mirror so your emotions may be different.

Suggestions for group setting

1. Have comfortable space between participants before starting.

2. Softly play music in the background while participants are writing down personal thoughts.

3. Reserve a place for private consultation, should the need arise.

   Have trained counselors or clergy present at all times.

timid

Rejection   saddened

Abuse   anxious   Parenting

abandoned   forgiveness

Neglected   inadequate   DESERTED

failure   depression   addiction

Loniliness   Insufficient

Disillusioned

Fear

What do you see?

Your Journal...

Write down what you see in the mirror.

_____

_____

_____

_____

_____

_____

_____

_____

_____

_____

_____

_____

_____

Affirmations

At this point, participants are to close their eyes, if comfortable enough to do so and relax. While the participants are relaxing, the instructor is to walk around the room and read the affirmations listed below to the class in a very soft voice.

Before you close this section of the exercise, it is vital that the affirmations are read. It brings the participants back to a safe place within themselves, while also returning to a better mind-set than before the exercise began.

It also gives the instructor the opportunity to address the class and make sure everyone is all right or if there are special needs that need to be met. For example, counseling, listening ear, or quiet time. It also gives the instructor time to remind them of their tools in their toolbox, which are valuable to them in case a memory comes up while away from class.

Words to be Read

You are beautiful,
You're perfect,
You're safe,
You're smart,
You're valuable,
You're awesome
You're loved,
You're needed,
You're necessary,
You're vital,

You're wanted,
You're needed,
You're powerful,
You're important.

Repeat three times, and then close!

Second Dimension of Reflection

Topic of Discussion

How do these topics of discussion apply to your message in the mirror?

I n this section, you will apply the following definitions from page 28 to the information you discovered about yourself in your mirror of reflection. You will see how your perception of things would have been different if they were active in your life. These definitions have a clinical viewpoint, applying directly to your inner self.

Utilize these definitions toward your personal journey, while reflecting on your view of the past and your present life. In doing so, you will discover how and why you view things the way you do. How you see things is important because it determines how you treat and respond to it.

On your journal page, write down that which applies to you, so you can get a clear picture of what's going on. Please remember you're in your process stage, so allow yourself a chance to breathe. This process will launch you into the next dimension of this exercise; make sure you take your time and do the journal page.

Definitions

1. *Session — Self-Reliance*
   Confidence in one's self, being self-sufficient

2. *Session — Independence*
   Freedom from dependence and control by another person or thing

3. *Session — Dependence*
   Leaning on something or someone

4. *Session — Journaling*
   The writing down of thought pattern

5. *Session — Balance*
   A state of emotional and mental stability, in which someone is calm and able to make rational decisions and judgements.

Topics of Discussion

How do these topics of discussion apply to your message in the mirror?

1. *Session—Self-Reliance*

   _____
   _____
   _____

2. *Session—Independence*

   _____
   _____
   _____

3. *Session—Dependence*

   _____
   _____
   _____

4. *Session—Journaling*

   _____
   _____
   _____

5. *Session—Balance*

   _____
   _____
   _____

Your Journal...

Write down how the definitions on page 28 apply to you.

_____

_____

_____

_____

_____

_____

_____

_____

_____

_____

_____

_____

Third Dimension of Reflection

Now what do you see?

As we address the third dimension, we will focus on how you view yourself now. This process will allow you to see who you really are. Even though this person went through trauma and pain, they survived. As you look into the perfectly clear mirror, see it as a fresh canvas that you can paint and design any way you want. You have control on what is placed in your mirror, what you have changed, and will be changing as you process. Remember you will be able to apply these tools to every area of your life. You also will have control on who will be painting on your canvas.

Now that you have your fresh canvas, what do you see? Do you see what I see? I see a strong, powerful person who found the courage to face their past, their hidden trauma by opening up that past closet, and facing those fears. Embrace the new you, you deserve it.

Take the next fifteen minutes to meditate on the clear mirror. Then, on your journaling page, write down what you see now. Please embrace this with courage. You should feel very good; you are on your way to the new you. Remember this is strictly about you, no one will see your mirror unless you want them to see it.

"Enjoy your journey!"

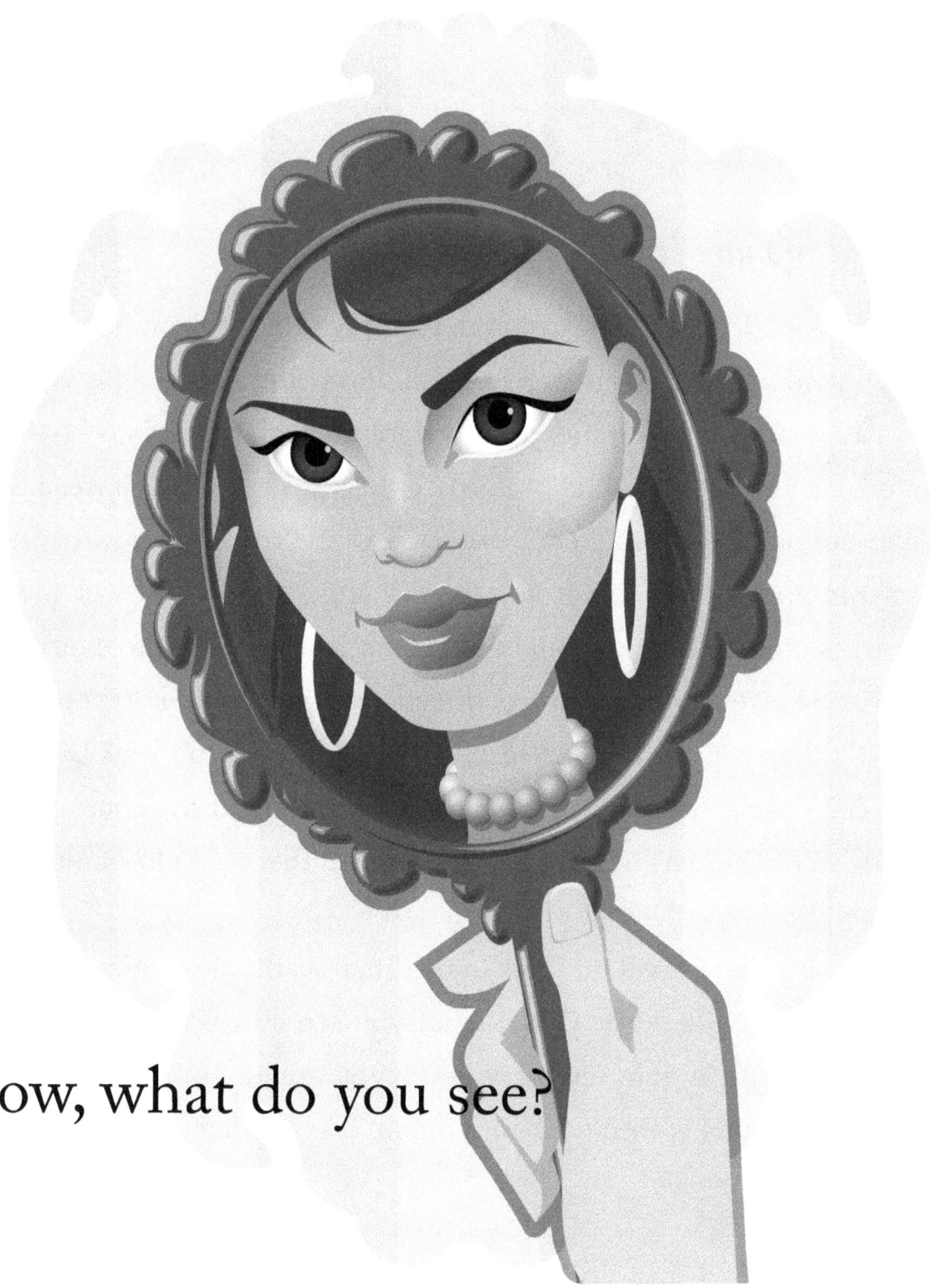

Now, what do you see?

Your Journal...

Write down how you see yourself now.

_____

_____

_____

_____

_____

_____

_____

_____

_____

_____

_____

Storm Sight

Exercise Two

Assessment

Storm Sight is an evaluation tool used to analyze another perception of your circumstances. Sometimes, because we are overwhelmed by our situations, we are unable to assess the problem correctly. The effect of this can cause us to not see clearly and, as a result, replay the same scenario, because we still haven't changed our perception of the Storm Sight.

Now that we have separated our emotions from who we really are, let's look at the circumstances of our storm that brought the trauma into our lives. It's important that we view the storm and analyze the cause factor that has us in turmoil.

As we address these assessments, I would like to use a meteorologist as a scenario. While watching the news, have you ever wondered why the newscaster covering a major storm would gather their equipment and run toward the storm? It always puzzled me that, with the information they had, they would not use it to stay away from the storm.

I discovered that through their training and information, they know a secret we don't know. They had learned to get close enough to the storm to gather the information and far enough to stay safe. In this exercise, we're going to get close enough to the storm — our trauma — to deal with it, but stay far enough away not to be tossed, again.

Death Divorce
job loss
illness INJURY

What tosses you?

Your Journal...

Write down your storms and how they are impacting your life.

_____

_____

_____

_____

_____

_____

_____

_____

_____

_____

_____

_____

_____

Storm Sight

Topics of Discussion #1

In this section, you will apply the following definitions from page 42 to the information you discovered about your circumstances in your Storm Sight. You will see how your perception would change when faced and challenged by the insight you have gained. Some of these definitions have clinical viewpoints, so it can be applied to your inner self.

If you utilize these definitions toward your personal journey, while exploring the application in lieu of the past and in your present life, you will discover how your circumstances and trauma affect your decision-making and how you react to life's situations.

On your journal page, write down which applies to you, so you can get a clear picture of what's going on. Please remember you're in your process stage, so allow yourself a chance to breathe.

This process will launch you into your next exercise. Make sure you take your time.

Topics of Discussion #2

How do these topics help you adjust your outlook into your storm?

1. Session – Beliefs

> *A mental acceptance without implying certitude or certainty on the part of the believer*

6. Session – Easing

> *To free from something that's painful*

7. Session – Estimation

> *Judgment, opinion, an act of estimate*

8. Session – Opinion

> *A belief stronger than impression and less strong than positive knowledge*

9. Session – Judgement

> *The process of forming an opinion or evaluation by discerning and comparing*

Topics of Discussion #3

1. *Session — Beliefs*

_____

_____

_____

2. *Session — Easing*

_____

_____

_____

3. *Session — Estimation*

_____

_____

_____

4. *Session — Opinion*

_____

_____

_____

5. *Session — Judgement*

_____

_____

_____

Walking in Sunshine

How do you feel?

Before we address this section, I would like to commend you for the courage and fortitude to make it this far. You have covered a lot of ground and the discovery has been very revealing. But, you didn't allow the pit stops on this journey to hinder you toward your destination. I am proud of you, but, most of all, I hope you are proud of yourself.

This journey is all about your healing and getting well, so you can embrace life on a level you have never lived before. As I stated earlier in this curriculum, trauma is hard to deal with and face, especially when it has gone years without detection. But, the power in this exercise, "Walking in Sunshine," is that it's never too late. You're a powerful and strong person. Stay focused and remember you're worth it.

Now that we're on the sunshine side of the storm, what have you gained and will adjust in your future? How has it helped you to see the storm in a different view? Take the next fifteen minutes to think about your new journey. Then, on your journal page, write down your new outlook. How will you view your storm?

Now celebrate your new journey.

WALKING IN SUNSHINE!

Your Journal...

Write down your new outlook on life.

_____

_____

_____

_____

_____

_____

_____

_____

_____

_____

_____

_____

Goal Setting

Exercise Three

Evaluation

Preview is an evaluation tool used to identify what mind-set is hindering you. We stop reaching for our goals when a stumbling block comes in and gives us a false report. We allow this interruption to hinder us from moving forward because of our past thought patterns

When we reassess our way of viewing our condition, we can see what we can do to change our surroundings and alter our situation. Goal setting can be hard to achieve, no matter your circumstances or your location. Sometimes, we think that because we come from a poverty-stricken background that we will not be able to succeed.

So, remember you have to do first thing's first. You have to realize that anything worth having is worth fighting for. Second, you have to know that what you want to achieve might be out of your reach right now, so you have to be willing to make the necessary sacrifices to align yourself with your vision.

Preview is designed to give you the necessary tools to get you on the road to your goal.

Exercise Three

Many people have dreams of goals and vision in their hearts and minds, but are too scared to embrace the thought of it coming to pass. With this mind-set, it makes it very difficult to gain the fortitude to bring it to pass.

There are several reasons this thought pattern could be present in a person. For example, education, history, age, economy, and so much more.

It is vital that a person first address the issue that caused the setback. Then reevaluate the circumstances surrounding it. This is important, because the person's perception might only perceive one way of obtaining their goal, where there could have been other avenues.

The question you need to ask yourself is, "What's stopping you?"

What's stopping you from going for what you are carrying inside of you? I know it's not easy, but you're worth it. You're in a safe environment to take the time to look at what's stopping you from achieving your goals. Take a look at Preview Goal Setting on page 61. There is a list of inventory and circumstances, but you might have your own.

Let's take a look.

Author's Testimony

"Life has given me another chance, and chance if taken can give me another life!"

Life can bring you many obstacles that make you feel bad about circumstances. Some of life's mishaps we bring on ourselves, other times life just deals you a bad hand.

The situations and choices you make can alter your mind-set. One of life's challenges that shifted my thought patterns consisted of my life sentence. It made me feel like my life was over; my self-worth was gone.

I believed I had no more chances at life, and life had made its own decision for me because of the bad choice I had made. I felt depressed and hopeless. Nothing good could possibly come out of my situation. I felt like I was in a pit and nothing, and no one, could help me.

I had to apply the Preview evaluation tools to help me out of the pit, which I felt entrapped me. By applying these tools to my life, I was able to give myself another chance at life, and realized that my circumstances could not hinder me from achieving my goals and purpose in life.

Instructions

Think of what's been stopping you from your goals in life. Now think of what you can do different to alter your thought pattern and perception.

Time Line

Take the next fifteen minutes to meditate on the goal setting exercise. Then, on Your Journal, write down the words from page 61 that applies to you. Please don't worry, no one is going to look at your paper, unless you want them to see it. This is your journey.

Suggestions for group setting

1. Have a comfortable space between participants before starting

2. Softly play music in the background while participants are writing down personal thoughts

3. Reserve a place for private consultation, should the need arise

4. Always have trained counselors or clergy present at all times

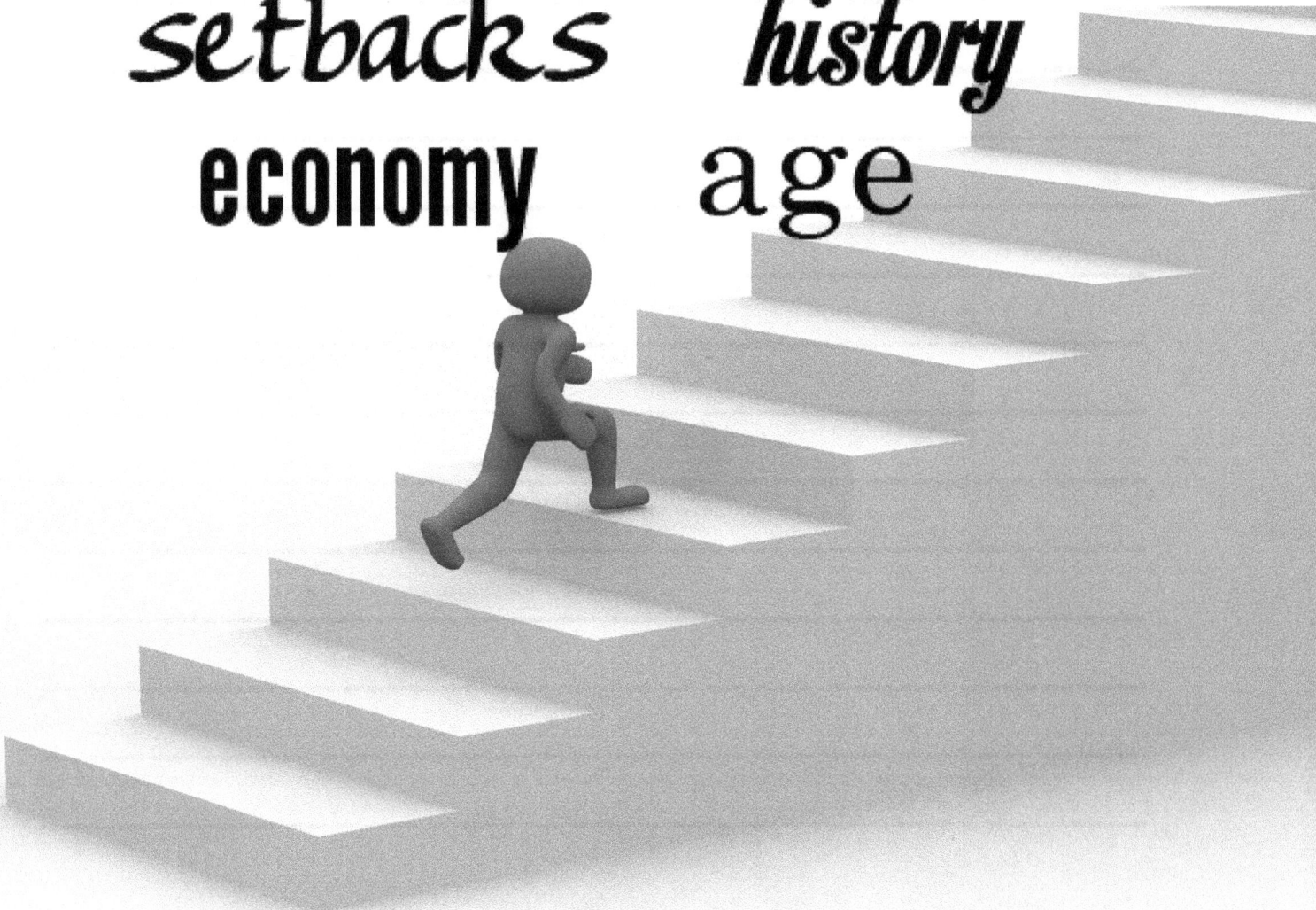

Your Journal...

Write down what's stopping you.

_____

_____

_____

_____

_____

_____

_____

_____

_____

_____

_____

_____

_____

_____

Topics of Discussion #1

In this section, you will apply the following definitions from page 65 to the information you discovered about your status in your goal setting, seeing how your perception will change your decision making process by the information you have gained. Some of these definitions have a clinical viewpoint, so it can be applied to your inner self.

If you utilize these definitions toward your personal journey, while exploring the application in view of the past and in your present life, you will discover how your circumstances and mind block affects your decision making.

On your journal page, write down that which applies to you, so you can get a clear picture of what's going on. Please remember you're in your own process stage, so allow yourself a chance to breathe.

These processes will launch you into your next exercise.

Topics of Discussion #2

How do these topics apply to you?

1. *Session – Self confidence*

   Confidence in one's self, and your own ability

2. *Session – Significance*

   The quality of having importance or being important

3. *Session – Merit*

   Deserving of reward and acknowledgment, a value that deserves respect

4. *Session – Value*

   What's important to me? Values to myself and others

5. *Session – Important*

   Valuable to me, importance of achieving goals

Topics of Discussion #3

1. *Session — Self-Confidence*

_____

_____

_____

2. *Session — Significance*

_____

_____

_____

3. *Session — Merit*

_____

_____

_____

4. *Session — Value*

_____

_____

_____

5. *Session — Importance*

_____

_____

_____

Your Journal...

Write down how the definitions from page 65 apply to you.

_____

_____

_____

_____

_____

_____

_____

_____

_____

_____

_____

_____

Review

You're on your way...

Before we address this section, I would like to first commend you on the courage to make it this far. You have covered a lot of ground and uncovered deep, hidden secret issues. But you didn't allow yourself to get discourage by your circumstances and roadblocks that was on your road. You're almost at the end of your process. I am proud of you. Be proud of yourself.

This journey is all about your destiny and legacy, so embrace it. My hope is that through my personal experience and heartaches, you will find strength, and courage to go on no matter what. Obstacles are a part of life no matter what side of the fence you are on. The key is to reevaluate your footsteps and mind-set. By applying the tools provided, you will be on your road to success. The circumstances that altered your journey to where you are doesn't matter. It's how you view your journey now.

Now that you're on your way, what new insight have you gained, and how will use it to adjust for the future? How has it helped you to view your obstacles? On Your Journal, write down your new vision for your future.

You can do it!

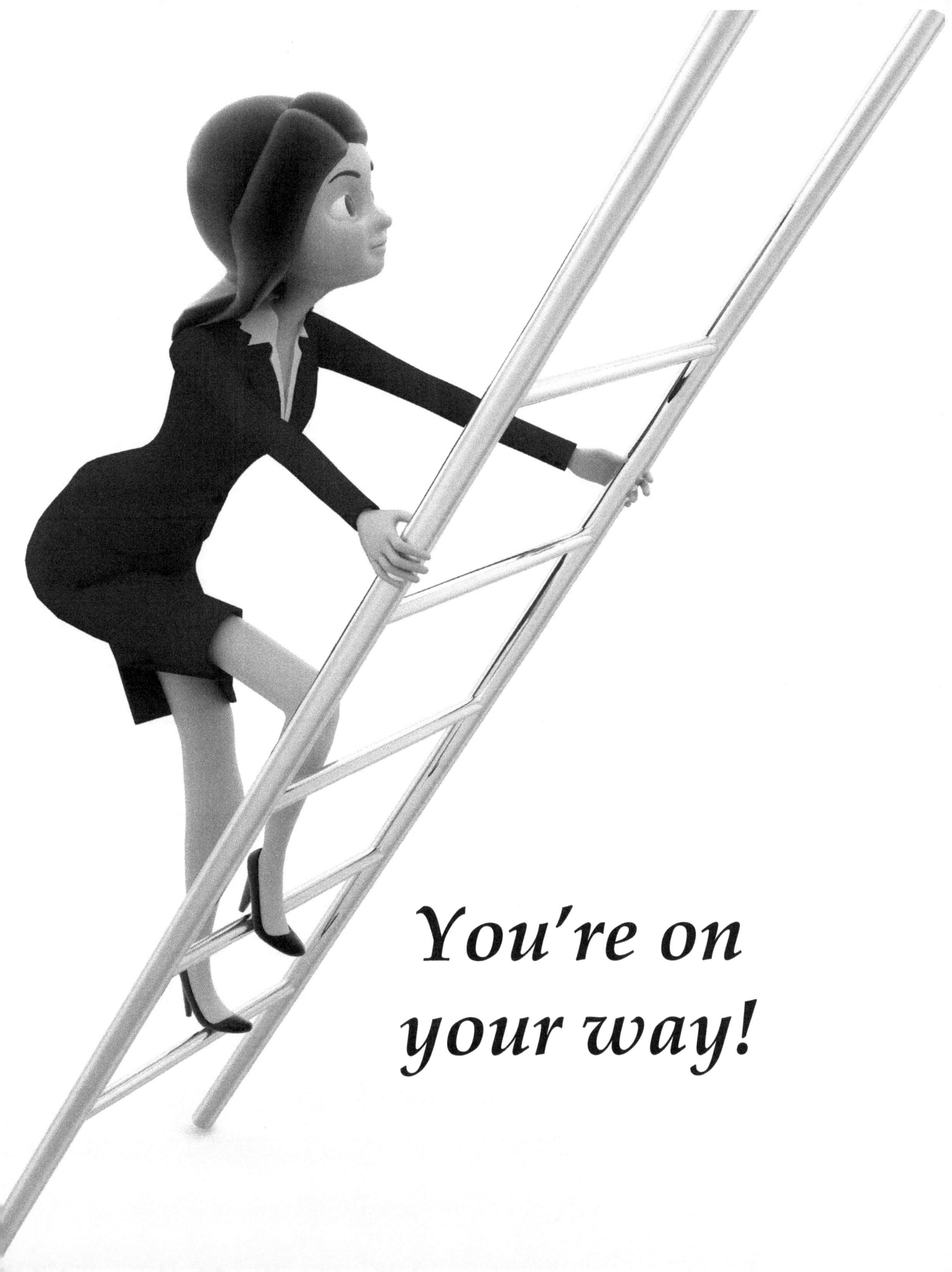

You're on your way!

Your Journal...

Write down your new vision for your future.

Doxology

Exercise Four

Exercise Four

Expressions of Doxology

This exercise is a tool used to bring you closer to your past, and start anew. So many times we are stagnated, we just won't let go. There are several reasons why we hold on to the past. One of the main reasons is we feel that if we let go there's nothing in our future. Our energy and efforts are in the past.

This is a false belief

There are new and exciting things awaiting you, if you would just let go. I know it's scary; it's going to take courage, but you have it. There are people, places, and things awaiting you. It's time to make a melody of your past, and write a new song for your future.

Expressing your past pains, disappointments, and griefs in a healthy manner is good. It's time to let go. In this exercise, you will express yourself through personal poetic word. Don't worry; it will be okay. Be patient with yourself.

Instructions

First, you're probably asking, "What is doxology?" Doxology is an expression of one's most deep and inner feelings. King David wrote a lot of doxologies in the Book of Psalm when his heart was broken, or when he was in fear and distress. Also, King David wrote Doxologies when he was rejoicing after, God had given him victory over his enemies.

I've written my doxology, so you could see what my inner self was processing during this time. Think about what you are going to release during this exercise, and how you want to say goodbye. This is a very difficult part, so don't worry how it will sound. This is about your heart.

Time Line

Take the next fifteen minutes to meditate on your doxology. Then, on Your Journal page, write down the words that are in your heart. Tell your past goodbye. Please don't worry, no one is going to look at your paper, unless you want them to. This is your journey.

Suggestions for Group Setting

1. Have a comfortable space between participants, before starting

2. Softly play music in the back ground while participants are writing down personal thoughts

3. Reserve a place for private consultation, should need arise

4. Always have trained counselors or clergy present at all times

Every Life, If Expressed, Will See Inside Their Own Doxology!

Hello! I know it's been a long time since you've seen me, and I know I look different now, but I've been through a lot of changes trying to stay alive inside of you somehow. I guess, for some of you, it's been seven to eight years, for other it's been nine or ten, but for me it's been twenty long years opression by my circumstances. It's a wonder I still know my name. I have been struck down in darkness, unable to see my purpose, my vision, my destiny, what was placed inside me. But, one morning, I woke up and there was mud under my feet. Because of hope, my circumstances turned from bitter to sweet. I started getting stronger and stronger, new strength I gained, in the pit I was standing strong, but my vision I've still not gained. I started looking inside myself. I couldn't believe what I had discovered. I saw rubies, diamonds, and sapphires. I promise you that at first glance you might not see, but give yourself a chance. You will find your vision, just wait and see. Then you will be able to write your own journey. Yes, in your life, when expressed, is your own doxology.

EXPRESSIONS OR DOXOLOGY

VISION

destiny freedom

hope ability future

power dreams

Your Journal...

Write your doxology — the words that are in your
heart.

_____

_____

_____

_____

_____

_____

_____

_____

_____

_____

_____

Topics of Discussion

Definitions

1. Session–Perception
A process of using the senses to acquire information about a situation

2. Session–Self-worth
Belief in one's self

3. Session–Method
A way of doing things

4. Session–Principles
Ethical standards and moral making decisions

5. Session–Blue Print
A plain of action, a guide to doing things

Topics of Discussion

1. *Session — Perception*

_____
_____
_____

2. *Session — Self-worth*

_____
_____
_____

3. *Session — Method*

_____
_____
_____

4. *Session — Principles*

_____
_____
_____

5. *Session — Blueprint*

_____
_____
_____

Your Journal...

Write down how the definitions from page 85 apply to you.

_____

_____

_____

_____

_____

_____

_____

_____

_____

_____

_____

_____

Expression of Doxology

Now that you're at the end of this program, your closing doxology will express how you feel about your complete process. You have been through a deep process and I must say, I am very proud of you! Pease remember that these tools can be used over and over. Revisit these tools any time you feel the need to do so and as often as necessary.

Congratulations!

"You made it!"

FACILITATOR'S

INSTRUCTIONS MANUAL

"Things don't just happen, they happen just."

– Dr. Johnnie Coleman

CONTENTS

Facilitators!

Welcome to the 'What Happened?' Program

Closing remarks from the Director included

When we face disappointments, challenges, and obstacles, the first thing we ask is, "Why me?" We don't always realize that things happen to us according to our dominant thoughts, words, and deeds. Even when we work really hard to keep ourselves in a positive frame of mind, things happen.

When events occur that we don't expect, they increase our faith, strengthen our ability to endure, and bring forth our hidden talents, abilities, and strengths. Why me? As Les Brown would ask, "Why not you? Would you like to recommend someone else?"

Why you? Because you can handle it. Because you really do know what to do. Because you need a little nudge every now and then to keep you on or put you back on track. So, the next time something happens to you, remember, things don't just happen. They happen the way they should, at just the right time, to the right people. Our job is to know we are equipped to handle it.

Divine order prevails in my mind and my life, right here, right now.

Dear Facilitator,

As a facilitator of this program, you must keep in the forfront of your mind that character and integrity is more important than persona and image.

We have been trained by society to put all our vigor into our looks and leaving our inside woman looking like a dead man's bones.

Definitions:

Character: Is who you are when no one's looking. Your moral fiber.

Integrity: Is demonstrated with honesty, truth, and honor.

Persona: Is what people think you are. It's what you appear to be others.

Image: Is a reflection of something or someone.

You might ask why this is important. It's important because persona might get you there, but only good character will keep you THERE. Wherever your THERE may be, from occupation to parole, your character and the maintenance of it is key to your success.

What Happened? seminar is designed to assist the community to desire a character development and an integrity interview. We must reintroduce them to their unique God-given design. "This is fearfully and wonderfully made."

But prior to doing this, we must first ask ourselves these important questions: Where are we? Where are we in our minds, body, and spirit?

This instruction manual is to keep you conscientious of yourself! Like previously stated, you have the personal knowledge, dialect, and appearance, but do you have the right spirit? It is your personal responsibility that your spirit be equipped in Him.

Introduction

The Heart of the Director

PSALM 23

There once was a Shakespearean actor who was known everywhere for his one-man shows of readings and recitations from the classics. He would always end his performance with a reading of Psalm 23.

Each night, without exception, as the actor began his recitation, "The Lord is my Shepherd, I shall not want," the crowd would listen attentively. And then, at the conclusion of Psalm 23, they would rise in thunderous applause in appreciation of the actor's incredible ability to bring the verse to life.

But one night, just before the actor was to offer his customary recital of Psalm 23, a young man from the audience spoke up. "Sir, do you mind if tonight I recite Psalm 23?"

The actor was quite taken aback by this unusual request, but he allowed the young man to come forward and stand front and center on the stage to recite Psalm 23, knowing that the ability of this unskilled youth would be no match for his own talent.

With a soft voice, the young man began to recite the words of Psalm 23. When he was finished, there was no applause. There was no standing ovation, as on other nights. All that could be heard was the sound of weeping. The audience had been so moved by the young man's recitation that every eye was full of tears.

Amazed by what he had heard, the actor said to the youth, "I don't understand. I have been performing Psalm 23 for years. I have a lifetime of experience and training, but I have never been able to move an audience as you have tonight. Tell me, what is your secret?"

The young man softly replied, "Well, sir, you know the Psalm...I know the Shepherd."

A message from Georgia Horton: *It is not by might nor by power but by the Spirit says the Lord.*

Tools for Success!

Insight

As a facilitator, you have to keep in mind that you will be dealing with people from all walks of life. The needs of the individual may vary depending on the individual. Culture awareness is necessary for success, so please read the cultural awareness information in this instruction manual.

Qualifications

To qualify as a facilitator of this program, one must have a love for people and a desire to put them first. Also remember that it's about the work. Each decision you make needs to be saturated with what is best for the improvement of the community.

Check-ins

Please keep in mind that check-ins by the supporting facilitators is essential to make sure the speaker is all right. Awareness of the psychological and emotional condition of the speaker could change during his or her facilitating and reprieve might be essential for refocusing.

Check-in signs do not have to consist of a direct interruption of the speaker. It would be a good idea for the facilitators to get together, and decide what their check-in signal may be. Check-in signs are also used in case there are other emergencies or mistakes being made. By having these helpful tools, it will guarantee a smoother class.

Format of Curriculum

Outline for Every Season

TOPICS OF DISCUSSION

1. Self-Reflection
2. Self-worth
3. Self Confidence

EVALUATION TOOLS

1. Mirrors of Reflections
2. Storm Sights
3. Goal Settings
4. Expressions Doxologies
5. Journaling

ROUND UP

Revision of overalll What Happened? Curriculum

Raising Awareness and Sensitivity to Cultural Diversity

As a facilitator, you have to keep in mind that you will be conversing with people from diverse walks of life. The needs of an individual may differ depending on the circumstances of a particular person. Raising the awareness of cultural diversity will allow you to meet the needs of the community in which you live.

Let's first look at the meaning of multicultural:

Relating to, or including several cultures. Also relating to a social or educational theory which encourages interest in many cultures within a society, rather than in only a mainstream culture.

Cultural Diversity:

We live and work in a society with people from different backgrounds. The languages, customs, values, manners, perceptions, social structures, decision making are different. To work effectively with others, you must recognize, understand, and accept diversity, as well as being mindful when you communicate with people from other backgrounds. It takes all of us to create a successful multicultural environment.

Work Effectively

To work effectively, you must recognize the barriers of communication. Cultural differences can be a communication barrier because it prevents or hinders an effective exchange of information. Once you know that, you can begin to overcome the challenges of communicating across cultures. It's important to remember that all people want to feel valued, respected, and understood. The challenge is to know what words or actions will be perceived as respectful and helpful.

Advantage in Ideas

Having additional ideas that you are able to select from is advantageous. Occasionally diversity causes resistance, because values, customs and mora] values can fluctuate from culture to culture. Ethical issues that arise can be quite complex, even though our world is becoming more multicultural, many different beliefs, codes of ethics, and ways of doing business are still to be looked into and changed.

Strategies for Communication

Now that you know how to approach communicating with someone from another culture, here are some specific suggestions to help you succeed.

Cross-Cultural Communication Does Take Extra Effort

1. Be adaptable.

2. Use your best English-speaking habits.

3. Do not use acronyms, slang, and jargon (don't use them even if the person you are communicating with speaks English fluently).

4. Be aware of cultural forms of non-verbal communication.

5. Recognize that people from cultures other than your own have different assumptions. (Research, or ask a reliable source for advice.)

6. Be careful about using humor. Save the humor for special times. Jokes are very difficult to understand for someone who doesn't know the language completely.

Enrichment Statement

What Happens? program believes in raising the awareness of the benefits of cultural diversity and its challenges in bridging the gap, and make the community we live in richer in awareness. How?

By asking and facing questions like:

1. Race and Ethnicity

2. Gender

3. Physical Abilities

4. Social Class

5. Age

6. Socio-economic Status

7. Religion

8. Personalities

Also stereotypes hinder understanding, although people within our group may have similar views.

Toolbox

Safety Locks

Safety Locks are tools utilized to give the participants assistance, in case, while they're away from class, a memory comes up. They are able to have some healthy ways to deal with the issue.

Below is a list of healthy ways to process whatever emotion you may go through.

1. *Take a walk or run in place*

2. *Listen to relaxing music*

3. *Read a book*

4. *Talk to a friend*

5. *Take a shower*

6. *Watch a movie*

TESTIMONIALS

Amity Foundation

when people gather with good intent

November 8, 2011
Board of Prison Hearing

Re: Georgia Horton W33911

To whom it may concern:

It is my pleasure to write this laudatory letter of support for Ms. Georgia Horton. I have found her to be reliable, trustworthy, innovative, and compassionate woman who is committed to ensuring that every woman who desires services throughout the institution receives some form of assistance. She facilitates groups, acts as a liaison between the church and women in the community, is a mentor, and a spiritual adviser to many.

It is because of her desire to be of service that she developed a Christian based self help group called "Girlfriend What Happened...." Ms. Horton has explained to me that she was inspired to create the "What happened" curriculum for the women to challenge their core beliefs about themselves, the world, and their future. The curriculum gives participants the opportunity to...

1. Recognize self-defeating thoughts & beliefs that are roadblocks to change
2. Learn essential skills to make positive lifestyle changes
3. Recognize how thoughts &core beliefs control feelings and behaviors
4. Explore skills that can improve thinking style
5. Learn how to manage uncomfortable feelings & thoughts

The ultimate hope of the curriculum is to empower women to focus on their legacy vs. their history. Through this present based approach women have reported feelings of hope, purpose, and acceptance of self.

As a result of the effectiveness of Ms. Horton's self help group she has been approved to facilitate the "Girlfriend What Happened" group at the Trauma

Amity Trauma Informed Substance Abuse Treatment (TI-SAT)-Central California Women's Facility (CCWF)
P.O. Box 1501 Chowchilla, California 93610
559.665.5531. ext. 7842
amityfdn.org

Informed Substance Abuse Treatment (TI-SAT) program. Over the past two years I have observed her ability to respectfully challenge participant's to heal beyond their past wounds. I have on many occasions witnessed her gift of truth free the hearts and minds of participants. She consistently offers words of compassion, wisdom, and hope. Her encouragement and honest guidance offers peaceful resolutions to many of the hurting women here at CCWF.

Over the years she has participated in, as well as facilitated many other groups. Through these various groups she has learned about herself and has worked on her personal issues as well. Most recently she has begun to work through the sorrow, guilt and remorse associated with her crime. Through her work in the Church and TI-SAT program, Ms. Horton has come to learn that there are various positive ways to cope with issues that have impacted her life. She has utilized the rehabilitative services offered at the institution to gain the insight and fortitude necessary to reclaim her life from the false and imposed limitations of the past.

If additional information is needed please contact me at 559.665.5531 ext. 7842.

G. Hobbs, MBA
Program Director- CCWF
Amity Foundation

Amity Trauma Informed Substance Abuse Treatment (TI-SAT)-Central California Women's Facility (CCWF)
P.O. Box 1501 Chowchilla, California 93610
559.665.5531. ext. 7842
amityfdn.org

State of California

Memorandum

Date : August 30, 2012

Department of Corrections and Rehabilitation
Central California Women's Facility

To : Board of Hearings

Subject : Parole Consideration regarding Inmate Horton, W-33911

This letter is in regard to Inmate Horton, W-33911. I have known Ms. Horton since 2010 when she first introduced, 'Girlfriend, What Happened?' to the Mental Health Department. The core of this curriculum is based on a foundation driven from Ms. Horton's own personal past trauma and abuse. The tools of 'these programs allow women to embrace how trauma and shame can be exposed without the stigma of reliving their past and instead by leading them into a healing journey.

Throughout personal therapy and progressive development, Ms. Horton has transformed her successful therapeutic discovery into an in depth series of 7-week seminars delving into the complexities of specific issues. These programs went from being sponsored by the mental health dept, to being implemented into their system, and is now apart of life skills 46b. These various curriculums relate to the struggles of overcoming past trauma and victimization, as well as the effects of the mind and heart. Currently, there are 7 different curriculums in session given weekly with final testing required for completion. Curriculum topics discussed include, but are not limited to:

- Vital Sign- Mindset
- Heart Beat- Anger Issues
- Two Sides- Childhood Issues
- Timeline- Health Issues

- Swap- Coping Skills
- What's Next- Goal Setting
- Exploring the Mind- Thought Patterns

I am consistently astounded by Ms. Horton's genuine passion to help those traumatized by sexual, emotional, and mental abuse using her own discovery of personal deliverance as tools and instruments to aid those who are seeking healing and liberation from their volatile history of abuse and neglect. When I think the curriculum couldn't be more effective, Ms. Horton steps out of her own comfort zone of healing, exposing herself to be continuously used as a vessel for therapeutic anchoring and encouragement. I pray you will consider Ms. Horton's undeniable breakthrough of insight and recovery from her own past abuse and see that she would be a valuable asset to her community and society.

Respectfully,

S. Freeman, LCSW
Mental Health Department

State of California
Interdisciplinary Progress Notes
CDCR 7230-MH (Rev. 07/11)

Department of Corrections and Rehabilitation

DATE	TIME	COMMENTS (USE S.O.A.P.E. FORMAT)
9/26/12	9:00	WHAT HAPPENED GROUP Attendance: Yes Participation: Full Participation
		Attendance: Content: Participation:
		Attendance: Content: Participation:
		Attendance: Content: Participation:
		Attendance: Content: Participation:

INSTITUTION
CCWF

CLINICIAN
S. Freeman, LCSW

BED NUMBER

| 1. Disability Code:
☐ TABE score ≤ 4.0
☐ DPH ☐ DPV ☐ LD
☐ DPS ☐ DNH
☐ DNS ☐ DDP
☒ Not Applicable
4. Comments: | 2. Accommodation:
☐ Additional time
☐ Equipment ☐ SLI
☐ Louder ☐ Slower
☒ Basic ☐ Transcribe
☐ Other* | 3. Effective Communication:
☒ P/I asked questions
☒ P/I summed information
Please check one:
☐ Not reached* ☒ Reached
*See chrono/notes | Inmate's Name (Last, First, MI), CDC Number, DOB |

Ms. Georgia Horton

PROFILE: Specializes in designing curriculum, coping skills, and programs geared toward the development and core needs of an individual assessment

'QUALIFICATIONS'

Designing Specialized Curriculums

- ❖ **What Happened-**   Self Awareness Course
- ❖ **Vital Signs-**   Mindset Course
- ❖ **Heart Beat-**   Anger Issue Course
- ❖ **Two Sides-**   Childhood Secrets Course
- ❖ **Timeline-**   Health Issues Course
- ❖ **Swap-**   Coping Skills Course
- ❖ **What's Next-**   Goal Setting Course
- ❖ **Exploring the Mind-** Thought Patterns Course

WORK EXPERIENCE:

CDCR – Program Development Facilitator of Life Skills

Mental Health-   CCCMS, Pre-Release, Inner persons group, lifer groups

Amity Drug Program Foundation-   Alumni groups, trauma based classes

Centerforce Health Services-   Community health awareness & cultural insight booth

Religious Programs-   Self-Awareness seminars, goal setting skills, counseling fire house

Facilitator Training-   Leadership-manual course, weekly reports

S. Freeman, LCSW
Mental Health Department

STATE OF CALIFORNIA- DEPARTMENT OF CORRECTIONS AND REHABILITATION ARNOLD SCHWARZENEGGER, Governor

IVISION OF ADULT INSTITUTIONS
Central California Women's Facility
P.O. Box 1501
23370 Road 22
Chowchilla, CA 93610-1501
(559) 665-5531 ex 7233

June 17, 2012

TO WHOM IT MAY CONCERN:

I am writing this letter to inform you that inmate Georgia Horton has been very active and faithful in attending many different Protestant Services and Bible Studies. Georgia has been involved in many self help groups. At this time, I was familiarizing myself with institutional policy and the structure of the Ministry Programs already in place. Ms. Horton was instructing a program called "What Happened" for the general population. She showed a great attitude and was very receptive to the changes taking place that comes with new management. Although there were temporary suspensions of programs of leadership and being a team player, she displayed integrity and tenaciously handled everything that came her way with authenticity and sincerity. Throughout all the adjustments, she continued to maintain her faithfulness to the congregation, Choir, and most importantly to the ministry as a whole, "What Happened" group is a group Georgia started years ago; her ássion is to get to the bottom of the problem that many inmates have been facing and create a solution. Many inmates have benefited from this program. Georgia has been working for me as a Porter in for the chapel for the past year.

It was these genuine qualities that prompted me to personally sponsor "What Happened, a self awareness course she developed using her own past and trauma as a basis for her curriculum. She openly shares her past and the journey that led her to acquire the tools and examples to which "What Happened" is composed of. I am confident in the program so much that I have given Ms. Horton the opportunity to expand the curriculum by establishing more seminars, facilitator workshops, and extensive time and ministry resources to further this worthy and exceptional course.

Ms. Horton is currently my porter here at the Chapel of Grace and has been employed since the beginning of 2011. I specifically offered the position to her because I recalled how she rose to the occasion when faced with challenging times and the remarkable way she interacts not only with demonstrate a unique and exceptional way of connecting with the hurt and pain the women are suffering and channeling her own past to help bring healing and insight to the women, giving them a hope, challenging them to be better and overcome their trauma. Her integrity and insight in overcoming the day to day adversities is not only commendable, she is a living example of true uprightness.

She is very dedicated in taking the teachings and advice inward, so she can make changes to her own mind and heart. She is a great help with encouraging others to work on themselves, as well. She has a great attitude in some very difficult circumstances. Other women here have expressed what a blessing she is to them.

Sincerely,

Chaplain Ed Crain, Sr
Protestant Chaplain

Testimonials

State of California

Department of Corrections and Rehabilitation
Central California Women's Facility

Memorandum

Date : April 24, 2012

To : Board of Parole Hearings

Subject : Parole Consideration for Georgia Horton, W-33911

I have known Ms. Horton for 8 years. She has been sincere and diligent in her spiritual growth. She has a genuine love for god with honesty and integrity to match. She has always welcomed me warmly, helping with chapel schedules, cleaning, and any other project that I needed help with. Ms. Horton is very respectful to me and my observation in the chapel is that she is mindful of her congregation and staff in general. She remains dedicated to helping those around her no matter what faith they are.

The Chapel services Native Americans, Jews, Protestants, Catholics, Asatrus, Wiccans, and Muslims. Although her spiritual beliefs and faith are firmly routed and very strong, she does not interfere nor impose her way of life with the different ministries. She is mindful and very aware of the different traditions and customs of those around her, respecting her peers with compassion and understanding.

I find her to be a remarkable woman with a heart that says she is always willing to listen and help. I have no doubt that if given a chance to enter back into society, Ms. Horton would not only be a productive member of her community, but would be an asset to society as a whole. I fully support her release. It is a pleasure to know Ms. Horton and I commend her for the positive impact she has made within the inside community.

Should you have any questions, I can be reached at ext. 7216.

F. BEARHEART,
NATIVE AMERICAN CHAPLAIN

Helping Out People Everyday Ministries

"Each 1 - 1 end 1"
Philippians 4:13

January 17, 2014

Valerie Frazier, CEO/Pastor
Helping Out People Everyday (H.O.P.E.) Ministries
1546 S. El Dorado Street
Stockton, CA 95206
Office: (209) 464-1731

Beyond Incarceration
Leadership Conference 2013

RE: Ms. Georgia Horton
c/o Whom It May Concern:

I am delighted to write a letter of appreciation on behalf of inmate and youth diversion specialist, Ms. Georgia Horton. I have known Georgia for more than five years. We met through a coop to reduce domestic and gang violence, sexual assault, substance abuse, while visiting California Department of Corrections and Rehabilitation (CDCR). I along with several other peace officers responsible for safer communities came to the prisons as participants in a volunteer *Beyond Incarceration Program* consisting of various law enforcement officials to include Judges, District Attorneys, Public Defenders, and business owners from San Joaquin County.

Beyond Incarceration was adopted by San Joaquin County Superior Courts *Community Collaboration Program*. It started in the county jail in 2004, and expanded in to CDCR prisons by 2006. In of June 2010 upon retiring from CDCR as a Parole Agent III of 25 years, Beyond Incarceration became a subsidiary of *Helping Out People Everyday (H.O.P.E.) Ministries*. We have the responsibility of community program maintenance to include coordinating the youth leadership conferences, routine communication with CDCR and other collaborate partners, quarterly visits, offender participation live-video feeds, video or telephone conference for planning youth events, written correspondence. The consistent communication builds the partnership relationship and training on public presentations, progress evaluations. The primary purpose of BIP is to increase safety and reduce recidivism by improving the quality of life for individuals who have entered the criminal justice system and at-risk youth exhibiting early symptoms of delinquency.

Helping Out People Everyday (H.O.P.E.) Ministries, a non-profit faith based organization with a goal to restore families to include youth and adults with a criminal history choosing to change their lives, through one act of kindness at a time. H.O.P.E. provide spiritual support as requested; self-help community based support when transitioning from state and local correctional settings; provide application, resume, dress for success attire, attitude adjustment support while seeking employment assistance; a women's support group focused on rebuilding damaged relationships with their families, a safe place to volunteer and perform community service work; opportunities for peer mentoring and tutoring; and a Cognitive Behavioral Intervention for Substance Abuse 39-week course, and a Common Sense Parenting 6-week class.

Testimonials

Ms. Georgia Horton, an offender residing at CCWF has come forward to share her testimony with her peers and youth when given the opportunity; she was chosen by correctional administrative staff when identified as a woman who had already begun to improve the quality of her life. She was in school, working a trade, staying out of trouble, which led to her participation in the Beyond Incarceration Program.

During one of the BIP in-house training presentations, Georgia gravitated to the M.O.T.H.E.R. *(Matters of the Heart Encourage Restoration)* Program. She literally took the few documents given and began building it to become one of CCWF's most spiritual uplifting programs. Now, it is shared with the other female offenders desiring to reconnect with their families.

To date, Georgia has been sharing her offense history and a reflection of the bad choices she made that led to her incarceration, with the hopes of deterring youth from making the same or similar mistakes. Her impact on the youth and adults during the live-video feed conversations are profound. She has participated in speaking to approximately 7,500 students *(up to 18 conferences with youth ranging in age from 12-18)* in the youth diversion program.

Since I have known Georgia, I have seen her become a youth diversion *specialist in domestic violence and sexual assault*. Her passion is felt all through each session. She serves as panelist and leader in helping new commitments entering the women's prison to make good choices although they have entered in to a correctional setting. Georgia assists in the interviews of women who express an interest in BIP to go above and beyond the expectations and commitments necessary to participate. Not only does Georgia give her time and heart, but she also provide monetary support along with other inmates who sponsor our Youth Conferences.

Should Ms. Georgia Horton be given the privilege to parole, may her work continue and become of greater relevance in the community. There are so many youth dying on our streets and far too many women suffering from mental illness, domestic violence and sexual assault. Georgia has demonstrated her humility and remorse for her criminal history continuously during the Youth Conferences as she is reminded and questioned by the audience about the role she played in someone losing their life. Her passion has made youth think about their choices as she highlights the consequences. Attached are articles that have been shared about Beyond Incarceration and the impact of how it contributes to changing the lives of self and others, through life-saving decisions being practiced everyday. Five years later, Georgia still proves to be the asset expected during her initial interview for Beyond Incarceration.

Should you have any further questions regarding Ms. Horton, please contact us.

Sincerely,

VALERIE FRAZIER
Chief Executive Officer/Pastor
Beyond Incarceration Program Director

RICHARD A. VLAVIANOS
Honorable Judge,
San Joaquin County Superior Court

ADMINISTRATION

1546 S. El Dorado Street
Stockton, CA 95206

Office/Fax: (209) 464-1731
www.hopeministries-bip.org

Above and Beyond

PRESENTED TO

GEORGIA HORTON

THANK YOU FOR YOUR OUTSTANDING CONTRIBUTIONS IN OUR
COMMUNITY AND FOR MAKING THE AMITY TI-SAT STAND ABOVE THE
REST.

Amity Foundation

_____
G. HOBBS, PROGRAM DIRECTOR

_____
P. MENDES, CCIII

August 25, 2010